Seeing Mission Fields in the Midst of Battlefields

Teresa Ann Criswell

Heavenly Wit: Seeing Mission Fields in the Midst of Battlefields

Copyright © 2017, 2018, 2019, 2020 by Teresa Ann Criswell
Triumphant Victory Publishing

www.LetsTalkStudio.com | www.GodlyChitChat.com

Cover Design by Alisa Hope Wagner | www.AlisaHopeWagner.com

Photo by Tristin Criswell | www.ParisKeelea.com

ISBN #: 9798608963827

Dedication

This book is dedicated to:
- My LORD as my fingers dance upon the keyboard, may this be an expression of my worship to YOU.

Then to:
- the reader, remember that you are HIS Masterpiece. You are God's treasured literary work. You are HIS unique treasure created to continuously point others forward and upward to The Father GOD.

- my beautiful family; especially my earthly hero and husband, Tim; my brilliant daughter Tristin; my compassionate son Cody, awesome daughter in love Jennifer as well as my beloved grandson, Nicholas Ray.

- my praying parents
- my sisters and their beautiful families
- my mother in love and brother in loves and their families
- my precious friends

- Lisa Bevere, thank you for imparting and speaking forth by the Spirit of GOD: "boldness and creativity" and "There are women in the room who were meant to write books" on March 14, 2004 –
I ran after My GOD ever since that time.

Introduction

At the end of the dark hallway within their high school there were teenagers taunting and surrounding a young girl. She was seemingly cornered and alone. Yet I was startled to realize the bravery that surrounded her spirit. She stood firm as the flippant accusations flew with seeming violence. Yet, this bold, fearless confidence from within allowed her to look straight onto her bullies like a steadied arrow. Those beautiful eyes revealing pinpoint accuracy of the vibrant joy that glimmered from her inner spirit. Raw hope and rare vibrancy pulsating through her every part.

While all this was taking place; it seemed she was leaning in, intently watching with fascination even as she experienced it first-hand. Her head leaned slightly to the right as though she were watching a suspenseful thriller.

Their insults were being morphed to do the opposite of what was intended; against its very nature to tear down. Instead of havoc there was this stirring of laughter and joy that caused the insults to have no penetrating power.

It didn't make sense as even my observations of what was happening caused my own blood to boil.

Bewildered. I sat there as I witnessed her eyes soften with supernatural compassion. It was in that moment I realized WHY their words had no power.

Amazingly enough she was choosing to hear GOD's divine WORDS of victorious life saturate her soul and mind right in the middle of it all. I could see more clearly that as the bullies shouted, ***there was a Divine Translator flipping their words with destiny and purpose*** as GOD spoke abundant blessings of WHO HE is. In the midst; those weapons were now rendered useless!

Those teenagers, without knowing it, their curses were exposing the authentic message; it was none other than GOD's message of promise and hope. This is when I realized what this book was for. The little girl I had seen in my mind represented me and you. GOD wants me to respond to HIM in the midst.

I believe and greatly hope that this will be a book of divine resolve to point you upward and yet inward to the Father GOD. A book that stirs you to hunger and thirst for HIM.

As this book is in your hands or even on your mobile device, may you catch the awe-inspiring jottings that seem random; yet far from happenstance; intentional ponderings of promise.

One thing I know for sure is that in the middle of writing this book, there was a stirring to face upward. **I realized in the moments of confusion it could no longer affect me to become useless; instead USEFUL!** The confusion no longer had power! Instead, I was allowing it to be used to draw me closer to my Father WHO constantly brings clarity to WHO HE IS, no matter how dimming the moments seem to be around me.

Those hard-pressing moments were turned to precious points of entry to GOD's wooing. The wooing that bids us to draw closer to HIM. Inspiration of WHO HE IS, stirring hope to ignite faith from within us to display GOD's victorious, uncommon wit.

This book for even myself has become a beneficial tool. A witty instrumental resource of inspiration. All the while it has inspired and taught me yet again to remember the SOURCE of ALL; the greatness of GOD.

To realize that I need to remain standing in not just a version or idea of "truth" of who I think HE is, but in HIM WHO IS TRUTH.

This book is much more than a "self-help" read; it's an echo of GOD's desire. I believe more than anything that GOD's desire for you and me is that the words on these pages reveal WHO the only TRUE HELPER is as you are pointed forward and upward to GOD HIMSELF, revealed by Jesus so magnificently through the power of Holy Spirit!

I pray as you read to the end of this book, you would see HIS mission fields in the midst of the battlefields; for this purpose: to point others forward and upward to HIM.

Table of Contents

Chapter 1
How Can Insults Work for Me?

I t was in 2006, while in my cozy bed with my comfy pillows surrounding me. I was lying down on my stomach while writing in my journal, that was the moment I took notice of the interestingly surprising jottings that were penned to paper.

The words I doodled were none other than profanities, like: *DORK, B*TCH, PSYCHO, CRAZY!* The Holy Spirit in that very moment was teaching me through a type of role play.

I know, you're probably thinking or even saying out loud, "What?"

"Role play?"

"This is unheard of and crazy."

And yes, let me tell you, at first I thought it was ridiculous too. Then I realized, it was crazy! Crazy AWESOME!

So, let me preface with the following: words of discouragement, death and name calling were a deep, weak, sensitive hot button for me as it would be for most. It seemed I allowed flippant comments to crush me. Here is the reality, if someone would have cursed me with a curse, I would have received it wholeheartedly and would have walked around curse ridden. There would have been excuses as to why I was a victim; it would have been easily justified.

As I've explained my jottings within my journal, it was Holy Spirit walking me through training of what to do when and if these words were hurled at me; and HE was showing me how to overcome. As in HIM, we are overcomers. It was incredible. He was teaching me how HE has the last word over my life even with these very words. I can use the weapons that were sent to be used against me, to now work for me.

As I continued writing, the Holy Spirit was illustrating how to see these awful words as a life-giving acrostic. He was showing me how to turn the weapons of the enemy into powerful tools to encourage myself while glorifying the LORD.

So here they are:

DORK

Daughter

Of the

Righteous

King

B*ITCH

Beautiful

Intelligent

Triumphant

Compassionate

Human being

PSYCHO

Praising daughter

Set apart

Yielded

Compassionate

Humble

Overwhelmed

CRAZY

Compassionate

Redeemed

Anointed

Zealous

Yielded to Holy Spirit

Isn't that incredible? When people insult us or call us names, they will be stunned to hear our comebacks. The powerful wit of GOD's abundant life giving words, in the form of heavenly, divinely uncommon, Holy Spirit wit. It's a glimpse of what "being above and not beneath" looks like!

Practical reflection and application:

- Ask GOD for HIS Holy Wit and be still for a moment.

- How have you gotten to know Jesus in the midst of name calling and insults from others?

- Being aware of The Holy Spirit, write that moment down and let GOD know you're willing to walk this out with HIM in Who HE is as Victory. Begin to "flip the script" with GOD's wisdom!

Chapter 2
"Why God?"

Although we have heard, read and even considerably "know" the truth in being above and not beneath; how do we practically live this out with GOD and HIS Truth?

I am learning in HIM how we wait through the hardships, the mishaps, the mayhem in life that can cause us to regress or thrive; whether we rise above or slip beneath the circumstances.

Considering our natural decline, often times there is a whirlwind within the mind that causes us to see everything but GOD. In these moments we can be subtly seduced away to the age old, selfish question, "Why God?"

An old memory greets me as I think about my own life. It was a moment when we seemed to be losing so much; monetarily speaking.

Years ago, while I sat in the middle of the guest room bed; depression was my new comfort. I had no desire to leave my house. Getting out of the house was a subtle yet loud reminder of all that I couldn't afford. At least that is what I told myself.

The everyday moments were filled with the yearning for night to come. It was incredibly difficult to do anything because of my circumstantial perspective. I focused on loss. My fix and gaze were on all that I lacked. My thoughts were on how I wasn't prosperous because I was comparing myself to those who seemed to be prospering.

There was even a moment I began to sulk. I wanted to make an investment in a certain energy stock that was seemingly lucrative and many were prospering; all the while we didn't have the money to invest.

I am laughing as I can still remember: the moment I opened my journal, not knowing what to write when suddenly I heard in my spirit, ***"Teresa, the greatest investment you can ever make are in people."***

It was the moment where the wind of GOD seemed to be felt again.

There was a divine pause.

A heavenly "Selah."

That was the moment when the divine shift of awakening began in my life. It was one of those monumental moments in which I awoke to the Kingdom perspective of The Spirit of GOD within me.

If you could just sit here for a moment and really understand what happened. In one moment I was blind and the next I could SUDDENLY see. The perspective shift was the miracle in and of itself.

A paradigm shift; a dimensional portal seemed to open. My eyes went from seeing lack to seeing with this "unheard of" kind of abundance.

Even more so I saw with clarity as I began to recount with great intentionality what I did have: from my husband and children, I had my friends and family, I had a church family filled with loving people; I was so wealthy beyond the monetary.

In the moments of questioning, it is the seemingly universal question that unintentionally becomes our mantra; "Why God?"

I believe it is accurate to say that you and I both have said it more times than we would like to admit. It is obvious that this question although just two words, have a demonstratively accusatory tone with much speculating, assuming and accusing that GOD has somehow forsaken us.

> We are tempted to say, "GOD did it to us." This is spoken from hurt, shock, disbelief; from a place of lack.

> These are the crucial moments where if not vigilant; we assume that HE caused it or allowed it and in this, there's no way He can exist; and if He does exist, then how dare HE?

> - OR -

> "How could HE allow this to happen?" In that, we assume HE doesn't care about us and HE's too far away, and in turn we unintentionally say HIS arm is

too short for what is going on in our lives.

Think about it...this two-word question of "Why GOD?" ensues judgement. Many times, this destructive mindset causes us to stay as a victim with many times a gritty stance of "rightfully so." Yet the *rightfully so's* in life keep us stuck or even cause us to regress as we further say with defiant accusations, "You could have stopped it, and You didn't. You..."

All the while, we unknowingly become toxic people; not just to ourselves but to others around us.

How do we change the narrative?

The narrative simply changes when we change our position from where we see.

Repositioning causes us to see from a different view.

Here's an example:

You're at a table in one of your favorite restaurants. This table that you sit at has four chairs that face different parts of the restaurant. The chair you sit on just happens to face the restrooms. It seems that every time someone opens the doors to either use the restroom or leave, you keep seeing the toilet. Yet you have a friend sitting at the same table, but their view from where their position is overlooks the beautiful stream that cascades around the restaurant. Think about it, you're at the same restaurant, the same table, with the same menu, same amount of money but where you sit changes your experience at the same exact place. If someone were to ask your friend how their experience was, they would most likely share how amazing it was. While your take on the same time and space are completely different.

It is the same with perspective.

However, with how we see, there must be intentionality in where we position ourselves. We even start asking the questions that induce life giving conversation. For instance, when I want to know how my daughter's day was at work, I have learned not to ask, "How was your day?" The reason for this is because there is a huge chance, she will answer with the good ol', "Fine." So instead, now I ask, "Tristin, while you were at work today, how did you get to make that place better?" This results in conversation versus superficial answers that are simply shallow.

We must ask questions that create depth; an excavation of sorts, to get to the gems within people that God placed within every person. It's that principle of the "deep calling to deep."

Our questions can create life changing results - good or bad.

So now as we ask the kind of questions that induce life giving answers, here's a great question to ask God:

> **"God, how can I help others from what I have been through?"**

This question "flips the script" from stepping out of the role as victim into our rightful place as victor. In our role as more than Conquerors we reveal this by OVERCOMING EVIL WITH GOOD! Turning our questions from "Why God?" to "God, how can I make my world better all the while revealing YOU as my Helper?"

Practical reflection and application:

- Is there a particular situation in your life where you can now surrender to the Father?

- Can you write down what it is?

- As you ask the Holy Spirit to highlight it to you; what is HE showing you?

Chapter 3
Your Struggles now Struggle

In chapter two we touched on overcoming evil with good! Friend, this is not a dumbed down cliché.

This is UNDENIABLE TRUTH
that slays giants; the

DEVASTATING WEAPON swiftly
demolishing the safe places of the
enemy; while revealing

BRILLIANT STRATEGY that
causes evil to regret they ever
rebelled against GOD!

Think about this...the Holy Spirit of GOD is **WHO we are possessed by** when we said, "YES" to Jesus as our Lord and Savior; the ONLY WAY TO GOD! HOLY SPIRIT our HELPER, TEACHER, COMFORTER causes me to type with violent joy!

As we overcome evil with good; those things we once struggled with, now struggle with Christ in us. However, as we live this life of victory from our position in Christ; let's be mindful that we are doing this as an act of worship and not doing this just to spite the naysayers and the enemy.

Here's the best way to explain the difference. Let's imagine someone told me that I would never be able to write a book. I take it in and the fire within me is fueled to prove them wrong. Not only am I going to prove them wrong, but I'm going to make sure I not only write just one book; but MANY books; all fueled by pride as it sounds something like this: "I'll show you." Even as I write, my flesh cheers that on and yet all the while when The Holy Spirit has me step back, the motive is rooted in none other than pride. Again, the flesh in me wants to justify it, yet God's Word trumps it all.

However, if we know anything about GOD, one of the things HE hates is pride; however, what HE LOVES is HUMILITY. Think about this, humility is rooted in trust. Humility doesn't react - it responds with rest. Rest and trust resulting in living a life of humility. It doesn't fight dirty; instead it submits itself. So, let's run that same scenario:

> Someone tells me that I would never be able to write a book. Immediately I see that person as a victim taken captive by the lies of pride. From that place I position myself to walk out with compassion and can say, "Okay. I'm sorry you see me that way. But I see you as someone who could be a help to so many. One day very soon you will be the one telling people like me what they can do whatever they put their hand to for God's glory, instead of what they can't do." As you speak this...you will feel fake, but it's truly FAITH rising up. Faith coupled with compassion. Then taking that word that was spoken to me and taking it to GOD who is

the Author and Finisher of my life and say, "God! What do you say about that? Was that the enemy revealing what I am really supposed to do? I laugh because GOD YOU are so good! Was he revealing that I am to write books? Lord! What do you say about this?"

From that place is where I want to write every book I am purposed to pen. It must come from a place of rest and trust because that is what GOD has lavishly intended.

When we begin to see every potential battlefield as a mission field; we no longer see from the perspective as a victim or to "show the enemy" instead it's doing everything as worship as we see as victors; who are more than conquerors in Christ Jesus!

Practical reflection and application:

- What have you seen as a battlefield that GOD is causing you now to see as a mission field?

- Share what excites you about this?

- Do you see how you're not doing this alone? Share how you see even more that God is your Ever-Present Help.

Chapter 4
Holy Coddler? OR Holy Comforter?

As Christians we often say, "I am more than a conqueror" and yet we are living as captives that are continuously being conquered by the past; or by the today's we can't handle and most commonly by the fears of tomorrow.

I'll give you an example of one of my own issues.

If you read my first book, *"God Is Enthralled By Your Beauty" Finally Looking Into The Mirror and Seeing What God Sees;* you read about how I allowed the insults as a little girl to mold me into the person I became. The insults and curses of my little world formed my actions, reactions and interactions within

so many relationships. It
especially caused me to see GOD
with thwarted view. Every choice
I made was from the perspective
of lack to constantly be on the
defense or to say, "The enemy is
attacking", instead of reminding
myself WHO was for me.

My past held me captive; I was unable to
"handle" my today's because I straddled in the
shame of the past and the fears of tomorrow. I
got stuck in life. My physical life aged with my
years and yet my mind remained stuck as that
little Kindergartner. Temper tantrums came in
different forms. Some may have called it bi-
polar; others may have called it ADD and those
close to me would have just said she's moody.
Yet all in all, these labels were all symptoms
from a mind tormented by sin and shame.

So how did I go and continue to live a life from
a place of captivity to a place of freedom? Let
me be very transparent, this is moment by
moment; it's more than daily. I have to say that
this is one of the most freeing things to write.

Let me first mention, I don't want
to walk in freedom without The

One Who is Freedom. Jesus
revealed by Holy Spirit is my
Deliverer and many times
throughout the day, HE is
continuously delivering me from
something. Whether it be a way
of thinking; or a *seeming* truth
that is truly a lie. This daily
process isn't painful anymore –
as HE is my Source of JOY.

Why is this? Because I'm reminded that I am
not alone, Holy Spirit is so present that every
moment is HIS opportunity to teach me as I
laugh at how easy it is to rest in HIM. The Holy
Spirit loves to teach Who He is. He is faithful to
show me what I can hand over and surrender
to HIM so He can show me how He's already
replaced it.

> "Beauty for ashes;
>
> oil of joy for mourning and the
>
> garment of praise for the spirit of
> heaviness."
>
> Isaiah 61:3

It is as though I can see someone right now,
reading this, who just lost someone so dear to
them. At one point in your life a heinous, awful

tragedy has come upon your life; a suddenly moment that seemed to change everything. You might even have triggers that go off in your mind and you feel like you are in a corner and truly believe that there is no way out, let alone even able to leave your house.

There may be some of you who do everything in your power to let go of the past; yet it could be a smell, a sound, a word, someone's body language or even someone's name that sets you back yet again. If any of these describe you...you are not alone. I am not just talking about other people who are going through similar things as you; but more than that...GOD is with YOU and that is why you are not alone!

As I sit here and write, my heart is experiencing this GODLY compassion for each of you. I feel as though I'm sitting around a table with people who look unscathed on the outside but have a story that even the greatest playwright could never fathom to write. Here's the difference maker: GOD is NOT the HOLY CODDLER; he is THE HOLY COMFORTER.

What would be the difference between the two? Well first, let's read the definition of both a coddler and a comforter.

Coddler *(Noun)* - Someone who pampers or spoils by excessive indulgence.

The transitive verb for the word **coddle**: to parboil, or soften by the heat of water.

Comforter *(Noun)* - One who administers comfort or consolation; one who strengthens and supports the mind in distress or danger.

The transitive verb for **Comfort** is:

1.) To strengthen; to invigorate; to cheer or enliven.

2.) To strengthen the mind when depressed or enfeebled; to console; to give new vigor to the spirits; to cheer, or relieve from depression, or trouble.

(Webster's 1828 English Dictionary)

So let us look at the difference between the two words and then we will go into the relational aspects with Holy Spirit.

If GOD were the HOLY CODDLER, which HE is not, but if HE was, this is what it may look like:

There would be no partnering with HIM. We would not have the ability to see GOD at work because HE has placed us in a corner, making us shut our eyes so we can't see ANYTHING. From the enemy's tactics to GOD'S VICTORIOUS advancement. All the while it is because we are busy being spoiled and pampered due to HIM not trusting in us to trust in HIM.

In all actuality, if HE coddled us, it would be due to HIM not trusting in HIMSELF.

Let me say it like this, someone who coddles, they do not trust themselves to pass onto another person to get the job done. The coddler doesn't trust in their own leadership ability to delegate to others not only a task, let alone the confidence to see that they will be imitated and represented with excellence.

If GOD coddled us, we would easily be squashed; not having the ability to learn how faithful HE is as HE spoils and pampers us because HE doesn't trust in us to trust in HIM. It would be a life of hearing something like this, "You sit over there in the corner while I fight for you but you'll never know my LOVE for you because I don't think you could handle trusting in Me. I don't want you to feel that I have failed you." Thank the LORD this is not WHO HE IS.

To keep going with that scenario is needless and I believe you got the point. So now let's go onto the glimpses of how we know WHO HE really is. Even while I attempt to write it down, it won't come close to the deep, vast revelation of WHO HE IS...realize that this is a mediocre attempt in comparison and yet still powerful.

The HOLY COMFORTER. WOW! Let that seep into your mind. God strengthens while invigorating us, cheering for us and causing us to be refreshed with new life in HIM. He strengthens the mind when depressed; HE consoles and gives new vigor to the spirit of a person; HIS presence lifts every presence of depression. He does all of this while saying, "Rise up! For the Glory of the LORD has risen upon you."

As we ARISE, it is not in who we are; but in WHO HE IS. When HE says to arise, HE is believing that we will in HIM. He knows WHO HE IS; and in this knowing of WHO HE IS, it makes me wonder if HE thinks, "If they only knew WHO I truly AM, they would arise and shine brighter than the most brilliant sun."

Friend, let's really get to know GOD, know HIM intimately. Know HIS scent, the rhythms of HIS heartbeat. Remember in the beginning of this chapter when I made mention of what some may be experiencing? To those who are seeing a therapist or on medications; the next time you go in or take your medication; as an activation, lift up that pill or pills and dedicate it to the Lord before taking it. Commit that time with the therapist to GOD as well. Let it be a faith step in the process; as though you are handing it over to GOD and say something like, "LORD, I am expecting that I am allowing you to continuously replace every hardship and difficulty, every mistake and betrayal, every trauma and regret; every haunting episode; every terror of night be turned over to YOU LORD and now become my sweet dreams of peace. And the PTSD that once stood for Post Traumatic Stress Disorder, I now proclaim as I am Persistently Trusting in my Savior Divine.

PTSD now stands for:

Persistently

Trusting in my

Savior

Divine

Now let the suddenlies of destruction be turned around as "suddenlies of divine dignity" in Jesus name. Every trigger that reminded you of hurt and shame, **may they now be triggers of your hope and joy in Christ Jesus.** Those things that bound you; they have lied to you for long enough as you now get to ARISE in WHO GOD IS.

He is cheering for you to trust in HIM as HE sees you as His Masterpiece. A masterpiece that can no longer be hidden but displayed with great worth and value.

In the middle of darkness may we see our opportunity to be the light! The light that helps us to let go of the past, realizing the power of GOD and how equipped we truly are in HIM.

Every daunting smell, sound, word, body language of the past be now the catapult that sends you running in HIS JOY and PEACE. Light to darkness; death to abundant life. Even in the moments you can't make sense of things; your sense of KNOWING that Christ Jesus continuously frees us of yesterday allows us to live in the present moments to simply yet profoundly SHINE by being the LIGHT!

Practical reflection and application:

- What triggers can you now give to GOD?

- How can you allow the triggers to now work for you versus against?

- What part of this chapter wooed you back to The Father?

Chapter 5

Arise! Shine!

"We were not meant to talk about how dark it is; we were simply meant to shine THE LIGHT of GOD in the midst of the darkness."

- Teresa Ann Criswell

But how? How do we not talk about the darkness and yet tackle it at the same time? This is the answer that is revealed through the lives of those who saw GOD's way of living was more important than their own; even unto death, for the cause of Christ.

Being the light requires the flesh and ego to die and the true spirit of GOD within us to arise, just as it says in Isaiah 60:1, "Arise! Shine! For the glory of the Lord has risen upon you." Why do we arise and shine? Because the glory of the

Lord has risen upon us, this is the only reason we can arise and shine...it's all because of God and His glory!

This is HOW we arise and shine, by:

Loving our enemies...but HOW?

Here it is:

- Being kind to the unkind.

- Doing good to those who hate us,

- Blessing those who curse us and

- Praying for those who hurt us.

- Overcoming evil with good;

- Living the GOD inspired life in the midst of evil.

So often we allow the evil to have the main narrative in our lives. For me, and I believe for many that are reading this, perhaps you are saying, "Enough is enough to this never-ending cycle that results in _____."

For instance, the world and the church alike recite this quote often, "Insanity is doing the same thing over and over again expecting different results."

If you have ever read the Book of Proverbs, this quote definitely falls in line with the many Proverbial scriptures pointing to what the foolish and the wise do. Yet the wise do the unconventional; they do the *peculiar* things; the things that cause the onlookers to sit and stand in awe and even say, "Why are they so different?"

This is how *we remain in the world but not be of it.*

These are simple truths that are incredibly profound. They point us forward to The Father and *His ways. Ways that are much higher than our own...it's the foolish things of the world that confound the wise."*

Proverbs 3:3-5, Luke 6:27-38, Romans 12:21 - I Peter 2:9-10, Romans 12:1-2, Isaiah 55:8-9, I Corinthians 1:18-27

Now that we know HOW to be the LIGHT; why is it important to be the light?

> For many reasons, one being that the *darker it gets, the brighter we must shine and most importantly because it is for the glory of GOD that our good deeds are seen among men...our good deeds point people to the Father. Our actions of faith revealed by God's love saves people's lives...it's all about God's VIOLENT LOVE displayed upon the Cross of Calvary.*

Here's another reason: it has to do with FAVOR. The favor, the anointing of GOD'S grace that is doused upon our lives is from the loyalty and kindness we wear as a necklace and never taking it off for anyone or anything, no matter what. It needs to be seared upon our hearts. When we live it out as though it were a **"must have"** accessory upon our lives, then the results of favor are by default...and the promise attached to this is that **you will** have favor with both God and man. **It's for the purpose of leaving traces of heaven**

wherever we go. It causes even our enemies to live at peace with us. Yes! The "Kingdom of God" kind of living is what invades the earth so we can make a way for GOD to have HIS way within people on this earth. The prayer that Jesus prayed, giving example to his disciples of how to pray, "Thy Kingdom come, thy will be done on earth as it is in heaven..." This is how we see heaven on earth; it's through our good works that show we believe GOD in the midst of unbelief.

Practical reflection and application:

- How is GOD showing you to be the light in your circle of influence?

- Has someone left traces of heaven upon your life? If so, who are they?

- Now that you have that person in the forefront of your mind, pray and declare the blessings of the LORD over their lives.

Philippians 2:15, Matthew 5:16, John 3
Proverbs 3:3-5, Proverbs 16:7, Matthew 6:9-13

Chapter 6
Leaving Traces

"Thy Kingdom come, thy will be done on earth as it is in heaven."

Leaving traces of GOD upon the earth. Our spheres of influence forever transformed by the touch you bring to their world.

With that said, what if we had everything we ever dreamed of? I know for me personally that if I had everything - pride would be the ruler of my life and it would be the blatant mindset of, "Good job! Look at you! You did everything the right way. Because you did your part, look how blessed you are." That self-righteous, "self-talk" stirs up pride.

Then on the other side of the pendulum, you're struggling in seemingly every way from health to financial with the condemning self-talk that says, "You must have done something wrong. Look at you, you're such a failure. Do you ever please GOD? Why do you even try? Your prayers aren't being answered because HE obviously doesn't hear you anymore."

What if both people worked just as hard? What if they both gave just as much as the other, yet one sees the "quote on quote" blessings and the other person sees hardship. This scenario must awaken us to never allow results be the mouthpiece for GOD. When you sit back and ponder these two sides, they both somehow "boast" in what "self" did or didn't do.

For some you may feel as though if you live a life of affliction and poverty then perhaps you are pleasing GOD. Or perhaps if you live a life of prosperity then you are somehow living the blessed life; or maybe if you are healthy then it's because you have done it all right. What about those people who did everything right health wise and now have cancer or a debilitating disease. What about those who don't do anything right health wise at and yet are seemingly well?

So often we have allowed our circumstances to tell us what GOD is or is not saying. Here is something we must remember...Circumstances are NOT GOD's spokesperson. Yet, no matter how comfortable we get either in our "comforts of much" or "discomforts of mayhem", GOD wants to be The ONE WHO IS TRULY OUR ONE AND ONLY GREAT COMFORT. HE wants us to know that HE has already approved of us before we did anything right or wrong. He loved us even while we were yet in the middle of sin.

What I'm about to address next is where the rubber meets the road. This is where many of us in America especially have the disconnect; this is where we think that if we sin or live a lifestyle of sin that HIS grace is still sufficient. Before we go any further, let me be very clear and concise:

> *His grace is not made available to excuse our sin; God's beautiful grace is made available to EMPOWER us to rise ABOVE it!*

For instance, when we live this life in Christ and we see things as an obligation; saying "we have to" or "we can't do that" because "I'm a Christian" then we have lost our love for The

One Who first loved us. When we're in awe of GOD, we'll do anything to show how much we appreciate and love HIM. Although our works do not save us; our works are evidence of our deep gratefulness to THE ONE Who did save us. There's this desire and "want" to do what is right because "we can" and we "get to" - not because we "have to".

Here's another part. Did you know the power of your tongue is a very important part of this life in Christ as well? We have the power to either send forth life or death? Some may be asking, what does the power of your tongue and sending forth life or death mean?

I am so glad you asked. So many of us focus on what is being said, however we need to peel it back even further. It goes back to Proverbs 4:23, our conversation reveals our heart, the conversation of our heart in how we see; it "tattles" on our mindset. To speak life is to be intentional with our conversations. Ensuring that no matter who hears us that it brings grace and peace to those hear it as recorded in Ephesians 4:29. Put more simply, it is to encourage, exhort, uplift and celebrate.

It reminds me of being in that quaint little cafe a few months ago near where I live. A couple of friends and myself met and as we came together, we ordered our lunch and coffees and just began a sweet dialogue. I can still remember when we were intently listening to one of our friends share some of her hardships; as we listened, GOD gave us opportunity to pour into and encourage her GOD's way in the midst. About twenty minutes into our conversation, this kind man, who was about to leave, hesitantly came over to our table. As he humbly stood over us, he kindly said, "I didn't mean to eaves drop, I just couldn't help but hear your all's conversation, and it was so encouraging. It is obvious you all are aware of GOD's love." He continued saying, "I am a pastor and curious to know where you all go to church." We briefly conversed while sitting there stunned with great encouragement. Little did we know that our conversation was revealing Who we were representing and it brought grace to that man who heard us.

Our speech, our conversation is another "get to" in the revealing of the glory of GOD.

Let me give an example on the other side. If my mindset is constantly seeing lack, my speech will follow my mind's lead. For instance, when we perceive from the lens of lack we speak lack.

When we see that we don't have enough; we speak just that.

Take it up another notch. When our mindset is cluttered with lack then we perceive ourselves and other people with little to no value; we might even see them as a bother; a liability; perhaps even "in the way"; not good enough; ultimately looking down on self and others. Yet more than all of this; our perception of GOD is placed within the confines of our small thinking. When we see with lack then we ultimately minimize Him in every way. Sometimes to the place where we say there's no way God could care or exist.

The remedy? Transformation. GOD's transforming power is what is needed and the key to that is getting the Word of God into us. Romans 12:1-2 says, "Do not be conformed to the world, but be transformed by the renewing of our minds..."

> The *how* to not being conformed
> is to be transformed by allowing
> The Word of GOD to reset
> perspective.

Another part to this is sensitivity and awareness of The Armor of GOD. Ephesians

47

6:11, "Put on the full armor of GOD". Notice it says, "Put on…" In other words: Consciously, deliberately wear the fullness of Who Christ is as HE is The TRUE Armor!

Our ultimate Companion, our great brother Jesus Christ is the reason we speak the language of abundant life. You want to speak the language that heals? Then let us choose intentional life-giving words to be the melody of our conversations. Allow God's Word of life to be heard through you like a rushing wind, revealing where we are truly from: citizens of heaven and only visitors upon the earth. It is a great reminder of how our time on earth is to reveal The Kingdom of GOD UPON the earth.

Practical reflection and application:

- How has this chapter caused you to be aware of The Holy Spirit?

- Does it excite you that HE actually lives within you to empower you with HIS grace?

- As you look back upon the traces of GOD's Ever-Present Help, how have you seen HIS abounding grace in your life that you may have overlooked?

Philippians 3:20; Ephesians 2:19

Chapter 7
Lack "lacks" Vision

"We want a king!" said the Israelites. Do you remember this? Whether you do or not, it is recorded in First Samuel chapters 8 through 15. This was during the time of when GOD appointed judges to rule as they were under GOD's authority. Can you imagine GOD being the leader over your nation and ousting HIM for a mere man?

Well that is exactly what happened as recorded in First Samuel. A mere man replacing GOD? The people begged for this nightmare, regressing exchange. Notice something, that was not a typo...truly regressing. GOD even in HIS kindness and mercy gives them warning of what will take place if HE gives them what they want.

Look at the warnings GOD gives and what the earthly king will do:

he will take your sons and
appoint them to his chariots
and to be his horsemen and to
run before his chariots.

he will appoint for himself
commanders of thousands and
commanders of fifties, and
some to plow his ground and to
reap his harvest, and to make
his implements of war and the
equipment of his chariots.

he will take your daughters to be
perfumers and cooks and
bakers.

he will take the best of your fields
and vineyards and olive
orchards and give them to his
servants.

he will take the tenth of your
grain and of your vineyards and
give it to his officers and to his
servants.

he will take your male servants
and female servants and the
best of your young men and
your donkeys, and put them to
his work.

he will take the tenth of your
flocks, and you shall be his
slaves.

In that day you will cry out
because of your king, whom
you have chosen for yourselves,
but the Lord will not answer
you in that day.

Yet with all the warnings, in my belief, it seems
like a glimpse of what would come thousands
of years later with JESUS about to be beaten
and before HIS sentence to lay HIS life down
on the Cross; the mob, the crowd hurled the
chants of spiritual wickedness..."CRUCIFY
HIM! CRUCIFY HIM!"

Let's go back to that moment when GOD warns
HIS people of what would come. Their evil
desires that blinded them to even hear, let
alone heed the warnings. The warnings of not
only their desires of today affecting them, but
also the generations to come.

Think about this, the two subtle things that
resulted from this unbelievable moment in
history were nothing other than comparison

and forgetfulness. These two things led them into the subtle traps which led to their infamous cry of, "We want a king."

Comparison led them to sow the seeds with misplaced belief. They "thought" they wanted what other nations had.

They had quickly forgotten what GOD had done. They didn't purpose in their hearts to remind themselves moment by moment of HIS new mercies that unfolded throughout their lives.

Gratefulness and praise were non-existent and it's what I call the *replacement principle*. I just looked it up to see if there is such a thing, and there is. It's imprinted throughout the Word of GOD, it's seen all throughout life. Even when GOD warned the people of what would happen if they got what they said they wanted, HE revealed this very principle. Psalm 1 is a great example to this among many throughout the Word. To me, it's the thread of GOD's LOVE over us. He is so merciful in the warnings. As though HE is asking, "Daughter, are you sure you want this?" "Son, do you know what you're really asking for?"

Here's an example of the replacement principle: The absence of life results in death. The absence of light results in darkness. Absence of gratefulness and praise results in complaints and poverty mindset.

I believe this is a key to life. We must see gratefulness and praise as FIRST an instrument of honoring GOD, which by default becomes a weapon against the enemy's advancements. The enemy can only have what we give him. He has to have permission, and his ability to get permission in what should have been a "DO NOT TRESPASS" zone is through our ungrateful hearts resulting in complaints.

I am reminded of the many moments that I read Psalm 100:4, "Enter into His gates with thanksgiving and into HIS courts with praise." Was the day that scripture jumped off the pages, grabbed my hand and led me to turn to Psalm 22:3, which declares that "...GOD inhabits the praises of HIS people." As soon as I read that I heard in my spirit, ***"If GOD inhabits the praises of HIS people then by default the enemy inhabits the complaints of a people."***

Practical reflection and application

- Who or what have you allowed to become the ruler of your life?

- Do you want to change that today?

- Share what you are grateful for about GOD and Who He is. It's a great way to get ideas on how you can be grateful for HIM even more every moment of the day.

Chapter 8
Deceleration or Acceleration

I n talking about the power of thanking and praising GOD, I just experienced a miracle as my big toe was seemingly crushed by a fire extinguisher that fell out of the cabinet onto my right foot!! My spirit began saying the name of Jesus as I winced violently in pain (Let me tell you, usually the last thing I am doing is saying his name 😳), but this time Holy Spirit had me put into practice what I've been led to write about; the miracles of praising Him. It is amazing as after I said His name over and over again, then my spirit received instruction to laugh on purpose as I praise Him and pray for anyone else that is going through this kind of pain and declaring their miracle as well.

As it began happening, I could hear me actually telling myself, "Teresa, you're healed. Your foot is covered in My Peace. You are healed." And not kidding - my foot at this very moment as I write is completely restored, then I heard,

"Activate what you've received by jogging in place. Now laugh. Give me your faith laugh."

I thought I was crazy and then as my husband would say, I was *"dumb enough to listen and smart enough to try it"* and began laughing some more and declaring Isaiah 53:4, 5 and then heard, "this is how you accelerate through the wilderness is with praise to Me."

Oh, wow God! I heard again what I wrote earlier, "As God inhabits the praises of His people; then by default the enemy inhabits the complaints of a people." I knew Praise was a must, but I know more of the why...

So often we know what to do, but we don't know how to get there and more importantly it is to know GOD more.

To get to the place of speaking life over those who are difficult to speak over; or to speak life into our seeming hopeless situations, the vehicle to get us to where we need to go is called the Grateful, Praise "Ferrari"...to thank GOD and praise HIM; not just stopping at praise but now being aware of His Holy presence. Realizing even more how signs and wonders follow us and to see them manifest is through the praise and to get to the praise is to remain grateful.

Gratefulness to Who GOD is, it is key as it allows praise to Who God is accelerate us through the wilderness whereas ungratefulness produces complaints and doing things the natural way as it causes us to decelerate, remain and even regress, causing us to remain in the wilderness much longer than God ever intended. I believe we are to go through it but not to do this life without HIM and most definitely not planting our flag there. We have the choice to determine whether it's the GOD intended eleven day journey or doing it our way for forty years or more!

Ungratefulness stirs complaints which stirs doubt and unbelief toward GOD causing our flesh to work by default in pride, worry, anxiety, anger, pointing the finger, judgement, focusing on the dirt in ourselves and others, etc.

YET

Gratefulness stirs praise which stirs faith toward God allowing Holy Spirit to produce love, joy, peace, patience, kindness, goodness, faithfulness, gentleness and self-control.

Practical reflection and application

- How can you begin exercising your trust in GOD within your daily moments?

- The best way is to remind yourself of how GREAT HE is. Speak how great HE is while you're working, in the car, doing dishes, cooking, while in the shower or taking a bath. Speaking to your children of how great HE is. Creating dialogue and conversation with them so now they'll be on the lookout to see and speak how great HE is.

- There's a reason: so that as your spirit which is infused by the Holy Spirit can now train your mind (renewal of the mind); which helps in accelerating your response time when things get hard and difficult. It is living out the promise of GOD recorded in Jeremiah 17:7-8 (Please read and reflect with Holy Spirit).

Chapter 9
What if?

As we talked about earlier in how gratefulness stirs praise and ungratefulness stirs complaints it leads me to think of the Israelites, yet again.

What if the Israelites were able to go back in time and experience their forty year journey into the eleven days GOD intended?

As we touched on it in chapter eight, so many of us know the Israelites grumbled and complained due to unbelief; but what was the stirring that led to unbelief? Often times we sum it up to their fears which led to the murmurings. However, let's go to the scripture from Proverbs 4:23 to go deeper. Here's what it says,

"Guard your heart with all diligence, for out of the heart flow the issues of life."

How do we know what the issues are in our lives? It is simply revealed when it comes out of us. It's like that saying goes, "When you get squeezed you find out what's on the inside of you."

Isn't that a fact? The issues of life that are revealed when it comes to complaining and grumbling is that it exposes an ungrateful heart. Think about that...when we are ungrateful; it will be demonstrated with how we think, what we say, what we do and how we treat others. So it is with gratefulness. If you catch yourself complaining, then simply flip it and begin being grateful and watch how it all unfolds.

Let's look at Proverbs 4:23 again, "Guard your heart above all else, for it determines the course of your life." Notice that word, "guard;" this word as defined by the 1828 Webster's Dictionary is to keep or preserve. In other words, "Keep, preserve your heart above all else, for it determines the course of your life."

When you are to guard, keep or preserve that means there is a natural tendency to abandon, desert, endanger, forget, and to give away. With that in mind, let's read that scripture with a flipped concept:

When we abandon, desert, and even endanger our hearts, our life's course will be a reflection as such.

So how do we guard our heart? How do we keep it? Are you ready? We simply, yet again get to be grateful to GOD for WHO HE IS. There is power to gratefulness. It is truly one of the greatest weapons.

Let's look at First Thessalonians 5:18…"Always be joyful. Never stop praying. Be thankful in all circumstances, for this is GOD's will for you who belong to Christ Jesus."

So look at this closely. Let's go deep with Holy Spirit. Holy Spirit, thank you for teaching us. Notice Paul uses absolutes in every part of this scripture.

How are we able to **always** be joyful? And how do we **never** stop praying? If that isn't asking for much, then how are we to be thankful in **ALL** circumstances? Really? Does GOD want us to be fake? So how do we live this life in Christ as Paul instructed with genuine hearts?

Are you ready? You have to look at much of Paul's writings as a maze. You start from the end and go backwards. So here we go:

When you belong to Christ Jesus, that belonging causes you to be so thankful to GOD that no matter the circumstances, we are in awe of HIM. Think about this. The awe causes us to never want to stop praying and in that because you live a life of praying you can't help but always be joyful. The thankfulness is stirred when we actually get the knowing that we belong to Christ Himself. Really ponder that. We are loved and known by the Most Famous One! How incredible is that?

Practical reflection and application

- If you were able to go back in time with the LORD, would you change your responses?

- What were the responses before and what would they be today?

- Did you know you can start today? Yes! It starts now by responding to the Father GOD versus reacting to the enemy.

Chapter 10
Resistance Fatigue?

Have you ever tried to resist something you really wanted? What about something you were craving? Did it seem the more you wanted it, the more you were consumed with the desire for it?

For instance, so often I have wanted to change my eating habits. Oh goodness...the more I thought and said, "I can't have sweets", the more I craved them.

The more I focused on what I couldn't have, the more I desired it. I noticed that the focus was where my perspective was and it stemmed from whether I was grateful or ungrateful. The same with focusing on not sinning, the more I focused on not sinning, the more I sinned, hence the awareness nudge to realize my lack of thankfulness for all that GOD has done. For from the place of thankfulness to GOD for

WHO HE IS, is when sin is no longer the focus because the goodness of GOD causes me to not want to sin.

This all leads me to James 4:7-8, "Submit/humble yourselves therefore to GOD, resist the devil and he will flee from you." Do you notice the key action in this scripture? What part do you see the most? Some of you reading this may be saying, "Resist the devil" while others may be saying, "the enemy will flee."

Let's notice something important... to resist the devil is not in the resistance; rather it is in our submission to GOD.

Really think on this - true resistance against sin and the enemy is not found in our ability to abstain and resist; it is in our adoration of GOD that we can't help but want to submit to GOD!

Can you imagine? I shake my head in disappointing awe. Most of my life I was living outside of HIM because I boasted in being exhausted due to my needless resistance against the enemy and wondered why I wasn't living a life of victory.

Yet all the while my boasting was to be in Christ WHO IS VICTORY.

Living in HIM reveals GOD's grace is more than enough, overflowing with supernatural refreshment as to live in Christ is gain. My awareness in HIM causes me to rejoice in this abundant life versus my awareness to sin causes me to walk in shame, making shameful choices. I have learned so much in realizing that this life in Christ is not about fighting for victory; it's about living from the place and position of VICTORY in Christ as HE Is VICTORY!

Practical reflection ad application

- How has resistance worked for you? Are you amazed that true resistance comes from submission/humbling yourself before GOD?

- Do you see how it isn't about your power or might but it's only by the Holy Spirit?

- Share how this revelation is helping you to no longer boast in your exhaustion; but boasting in GOD's overflowing refreshing power even in the midst?

Chapter 11
Submission Has A Mission

Reflecting back on chapter ten, resistance is the **result,** it's not the actual doing. You may be wondering, "What does that mean?" Think about it, so often we try to "do" the result instead of allowing the result to just take place by doing our part of submitting to GOD.

For instance, one of our pastors shared a great analogy of him saying, "Yes" to one woman being his beautiful wife. His "Yes" to his wife was the "No" to all the other women. He didn't have to go around to all the women in the world and say, "No! No! No!" I'm laughing as I write this, because it is so obvious that it was in his "Yes" to his wife that resulted in the no without even having to say, "No" to everyone else. Have you noticed we put so much emphasis on what we can't do versus what we "get to" do in this life in Christ?

We can't do drugs anymore; we can't watch porn anymore; we can't hang out with those people in those places anymore. That's like saying, "I can't go to prison anymore." How ridiculous does that sound, right? Instead we get to change our perception and our lingo follows with: "I get to be free of the bondage of drugs;" "I get to be free of being bound to pornography;" "I get to be free of bad influences and now I get to be the one influencing others to be free in Christ Jesus!"

In all of this I am led to the word, submission. Turn this one word into two separate words and you will find "sub" and then "mission." When I think of the word "sub," I first think of a yummy hoagie with potato chips and a fresh poured Coke over crystal clear ice. Oh my goodness, I'm already distracting myself.

Sorry, with all kidding aside though, when I see the prefix "sub," I actually see the word "submerge." When we submerge into the depths of GOD's heart, we see the mission and it is overflowing with victorious freedom, hence what I believe submission truly is.

Well, being that the mission of GOD is overflowing with victorious freedom which is WHO HE IS, then what is the mission of GOD?

I believe it is laid out throughout the WORD OF GOD...it's simply to intimately know GOD more and more so in knowing HIM we can live HIS will; living out HIS dream (As my friend Celina says), for the world to be lived through us so it spreads like a wildfire for HIS dream to be lived through them. HIS WILL, was what JESUS preached, especially the forty days after HE resurrected. According to Acts 1, HE imparted and preached the KINGDOM OF GOD! Yet practically speaking, what does the KINGDOM OF GOD look like? Again, its strewn throughout the WORD OF GOD. Micah 6:8 sums it up best, "To love mercy, to do justly and to walk humbly before our GOD." With that being said, humility assists us in our submerging into GOD's heart so we can live out HIS mission which is to do justly and to love mercy. Yet, to walk humbly results in doing justly and loving mercy, but how? Well that's revealed in so many parts of the Word of GOD. What we would do for those we love, we get to do for those who have hurt us, betrayed us, persecuted us and even used us. What?!?! Yes! This is when it all counts. This is when the KINGDOM OF GOD is recognized. This is what not showing favoritism looks like. Have you always wanted to know what it looked like not be partial to others? Well, this is how. Here are a few references to what the KINGDOM OF GOD looks like and how we can stir it out of us by finally submerging into the heart of GOD to reveal HIS mission:

"If your enemies are hungry, give them food to eat, if they are thirsty, give them water to drink. You will heap burning coals of shame on their heads, and the LORD will reward you." - Proverbs 25:21-22

"A gentle answer turns away wrath, but grevious words stir up anger." - Proverbs 15:1

"God blesses you when people mock you and persecute you and lie about you and say all sorts of evil things against you because you are MY followers. Be HAPPY about it! Be VERY GLAD! Here's why, because a great reward awaits you in heaven...You are the salt of the earth...you are the light of the world - like a city set on a hilltop that cannot be hidden. When we rejoice in and are happy for being mocked, persecuted and lied about that is a good deed shining out for all to see for a purpose, so that everyone will praise your Heavenly Father." - Matthew 5:13-16

"You have the heard the law that says, 'Love your neighbor and hate your enemy. But I say, Love your enemies! Pray for those who persecute you! In that way, you will be acting as true children of your Father in heaven. For HE gives sunlight to both the evil and the good, and he sends rain on the just and the unjust alike. If you love only those who love you, what reward is there for that? Even corrupt tax collectors do that much. If you are kind only to your friends, how are you different than anyone else? Even pagans do that. But you are to be perfect, even as your Father in heaven is perfect."   - Matthew 5:43-48

"Whoever wants to be first must take last place and be the servant of everyone else." - Mark 9:35

"But to you who are willing to listen, I say, **"Love your enemies!" This is how...do good to those who hate you. Bless those who curse you. Pray for those who hurt you...***if you love only those who love you, why should you get credit for that? Even sinners love those who love them! And if you do good only to those who do good to you, why should you get credit? Even sinners do that much!*

And if you lend money to those who can repay you, why should you get credit? Even sinners will lend to other sinner for a full return. Love your enemies! Do good to them. Lend to them without expecting to be repaid. Then your reward from heaven will be very great, and you will truly be representing as children of the Most High, for HE is kind to those who are ungrateful and wicked. You must be compassionate, just as your Father is compassionate, as this is the only way it works." - Luke 6:27-38

"Don't just pretend to love others. Really love them. Hate what is wrong. Hold tightly to what is good. Love each other with genuine affection, and take delight in honoring each other. Never be lazy, but work hard and serve the LORD enthusiastically. Rejoice in our confident hope. Be patient in trouble, and keep on praying. When GOD's people are in need, be ready to help them. Always be eager to practice hospitality. Bless those who persecute you. Don't curse them; pray that GOD will bless them. Be happy with those who are happy, and weep with those who weep. Live in harmony with each other. Don't be too proud to enjoy the company of ordinary people. And don't think you know it all. Never pay back

evil with more evil. Do things in such a way that everyone can see you are honorable. Do all that you can to live in peace with everyone. Dear friends, never take revenge. Leave that to the righteous anger of GOD. For the Scriptures say, "I will take revenge; I will pay them back," says the LORD. Instead, if your enemies are hungry, feed them. If they are thirsty, give them something to drink. In doing this, you will heap burning coals of shame on their heads" Don't let evil conquer you, but conquer evil by doing good." - Romans 12:9-21

"If you give special attention and a good seat to the rich person, but you say to the poor one, "Stand over there, or else sit on the floor" - well doesn't this discrimination show that your judgments are guided by evil motives? Listen to me, dear brothers and sisters. Hasn't GOD chosen the poor in this world to be rich in faith? Aren't they the ones who will inherit the Kingdom HE promised to those who love HIM?" - James 2:2-7

Do you see more clearly what the Kingdom of GOD looks like? The KINGDOM is within us, as it is not just a thing or a place, but it's the person of WHOM possesses us! We reveal the KINGDOM of GOD by releasing WHO we have freely received, and from HIM we freely give! We give because we love the ONE who first loved us! We give because we can; not because it's a have to...we give as it gushes forth from a place of gratefulness from THE SOURCE WHO IS LOVE in which we have freely received!

Practical reflection and application:

- What part of this chapter has awakened you to the magnificence of Who GOD is?

- How can you moment by moment express your gratefulness to GOD after reading this chapter?

- This is a moment to saturate in HIS presence. As you quiet yourself before HIM; open up discussion what HE spoken to each of you.

Chapter 12
Who To Wear

Have you ever noticed the celebrities that walk down the red carpet? Whether it be an award show or a formal event? What is the most common thing the reporters mostly seem to ask? It's usually something like, **"Who are you wearing?"**

Most of the time, when I hear the designer's name, and if I know anything about the designer, I'll say, "Yes...that's them for sure."

Why is that? I believe it is because the designer has a unique signature look that points back to the expression of who they are.

In that, it reminds me to not just wear what I want, but to be mindful that more importantly I must wear HIS brand which is LOVE so that others who ask are pointed forward and upward to HIM. All in all, the wardrobe is incredibly important. It really is. Think about it, especially within the culture of the Kingdom of GOD...we get to be personally clothed by GOD HIMSELF. He is truly the greatest designer of ALL...ALMIGHTY GOD! There is no way we can wear the old, ripped garments of despair while saying we want to bring hope by pointing others to the Father GOD! It doesn't work that way. Those old garments only point to our past hurts, past experiences and ultimately it points to self or those that hurt us. What and Who we wear is profoundly necessary and monumental.

So with all this in mind, what do we get to wear? We get to clothe and wear GOD'S love. As soon as you see it; you know it's HIS genuine love and not a faux or counterfeit. Compassion coupled with goodness points to GOD and HIS saving grace!

I love the KINGDOM CULTURE. Think about it. It does everything the opposite of how we would want to react. GOD'S CULTURE SAYS:

- See mission fields in the midst of battlefields.

- See those who have hurt you as your assignment to pray for them.

- Be hurt for them as GOD is instead of being hurt by them (Todd White).

- Overcome evil with good and this is how:

- Do good to them,

- Pray for them and

- Bless them.

Practical reflection and application

- To realize we were created to overcome evil with good, what practical ways came alive to you after reading this chapter?

- How can you reveal GOD today to those who have hurt you?

- As GOD is The Source of Light within us; share how you can shine the Light of GOD's love into the dark places.

Chapter 13
Full Circle

A few years ago, while in the classroom, my daughter was confronted by a bully. He made fun of her looks and said she looked Asian. In that moment she stopped him and in a steady tone she said, "Wait! You think I look Asian?" With some hesitation his tone lowered as he said, "Yes".

Seconds seemed to pass quickly as quietness swept over the moment when she clapped her hands against her cheeks and gasped with joy, cheering, "Thank you! I have always wanted to look Asian; no one has ever told me that before."

The boy utterly confused; the one who was once considered a bully, completely caught off guard. He didn't know what to do. No one had ever taken one of his insults as a compliment. He had plenty to spare; yet in that moment, he had this feeling that took over him that felt different. Without knowing it he actually had this moment of realizing that it was nice to make other people feel good about themselves. Wit from a heavenly perspective caused the bully to become my daughter's friend.

Heavenly Wit comes from that place of GOD's overflowing joy. It is a knowing that the Strength of GOD can see GOD's grace that empowers and changes the lives of others who least expect it.

There's this divine comedic relief resounding with the JOY OF THE LORD. The insults were instruments that prodded and poked at the insecurity from deep within. Yet when those insecurities are surrendered to GOD, those nerves that sent messages of pain to that area of the heart; it now sends reminder messages of GOD's hilarious healing and divine wholeness.

God's Wit causes us to be divinely distracted away from the distractions of this life. We now get divinely distracted by the greatness of GOD instead.

This witty life in Christ is not about spite and getting back at the enemy; it's not about getting back at other people. This is simply getting to grow more into the likeness of Christ and agreeing with GOD...pleasing HIM with our every affections. In this focus on HIM, by default it defeats the enemy.

What we once saw as an attack - we see purposeful assignments to go hard after GOD.

When we see the seducer at work within someone's life, we declare that their true assignment is revealed as having the gift to woo others with the goodness of GOD.

When we see and even experience a gossiper who spreads rumors about others...we declare with GOD's love, without offense how their true assignment is revealed as a herald of the gospel of Christ and one who spreads the good news of all that GOD has done!

When we see and even experience someone who is impure; we call forth and declare the true assignment of GOD over their lives. We declare they are coming into their rightful place of GOD to walk in HIS holiness so they experience the wholeness of GOD.

When we see the rebellious generation rise up; we begin to praise GOD that the rebellion within their hearts be touched by the LOVE OF

GOD and now be used to rebel against sin and use that rebellion to stand firm in Christ to not be moved by anyone or anything!

Uncommon, divine, heavenly wit...it's the way we can live everyday in Christ Jesus. This is how we become a spectacle in the most glorious way.

You and I have a once in a lifetime opportunity to point others "forward" to the Father by being light to the darkness; being breakthrough to someone's wall; being a bridge to the great divide; being salt to the world; and being beauty to the ashes by overcoming evil with good!

In this way of living, with GOD's Heavenly Wit; we will finally live as sojourners instead of living as permanent residents. Experiencing this life in Christ as ambassadors, missionaries from heaven; seeing mission fields in the midst of the battlefields.

Your story in Him continues...stay within the story line of HIS divine wit!

Practical reflection and application:

- After reading this book, how can you see your everyday moments as a mission field?

- Did you know that GOD isn't scared? I know that sounds absurd; but think about it. GOD is NOT scared what tries to scare you. HE is your HOPE and HE trusts HIMSELF so much that HE trusts you will trust HIM with your everything.

- Share with the group how this changes your mindset even in being scared and GOD not being afraid.

- How does this change your mindset?

- Does this book make you want more of GOD? Or does it just cause you to want to know how to overcome?

- There is purpose to that last question: when you want GOD more and when we learn more of WHO HE IS, we can't help but to overcome in HIM. This isn't about getting a promise and walking it out alone and then meeting up with HIM later when we need more advice. The intent of the writing of this book was to impart intimacy and to cultivate the revelation that you are IN CHRIST. That in and itself is so deep.

- This life in Christ is not just about being next to HIM, or Christ coming alongside us...it is by the power of Holy Spirit and knowing HE is our EVERYTHING; HE is our Source of Breath and Living.

More Questions to Ponder

- Are you beginning to see the incredible miracle of what it actually means to have the Holy Spirit of GOD living within you?

- Does it fill you with JOY knowing how witty GOD is?

- Share your insights on how HE has made you wittier even to insults.

- The GOD of the many universes is within us upon our receiving Jesus as LORD and Savior. Share how this rocks your world as you really reflect on that truth.

- How have you seen HIS abounding grace in your life that you may have overlooked?

- Please share with your group how GOD stirred you to desire HIM more as you read this book. Was there a moment that ripped down the old way of thinking even toward HIM?

About the Author

Teresa Ann is a joyful encourager as a daughter of GOD, who enjoys writing, drawing, painting and hysterically laughing with friends and family. She married the love of her life; who raised two children who are now grown as they are now grandparents to their beloved Nicholas Ray. In addition to all of that, she has so much fun being the YouTube and podcast host of, *Let's Talk with Teresa Ann,* with her weekly episode, *Flipping the Script Monday.* She also co-hosts with her daughter an inspiring mother daughter podcast, *OH...Teresa and Tristin!* Teresa is also an award-winning writer, self-published author and blogger. She is also part of the incredibly unique, *Godly ChitChat* Ministry with life long friend, Celina Baginski, who is the owner/founder of *Pearls In Bloom* and *Godly Chitchat*.

Teresa's passion is to come alongside women of every generation to encourage GOD's Truth to be rooted in each of their hearts with God Who is love. She also loves to convey how our lives are to be a sign, wonder and miracle that point others to the Father GOD as HE "flips the script", to no longer see from the place of lack but with GOD's abundant life.

Links:

www.LetsTalkStudio.com | www.TriumphantVictoriousReminders.com | www.ThePeeDiariesOfALaughingMom.wordpress.com | www.GodlyChitChat.com | www.AlisaHopeWagner.com | www.PearlsInBloom.com |

Instagram:

@Lets_Talk_Studio | @OH_Podcast

If you enjoyed reading this book, please leave a review on Amazon and/or Goodreads. Your words will help other readers to walk in *Heavenly Wit* so that they too can see mission fields in the midst of battlefields.

Here are a few other books that Teresa Ann has contributed to and authored. Make sure you go to Amazon to check out these other titles as two of them are award winners:

Made in the USA
Monee, IL
26 February 2020